101
QUESTIONS ABOUT NATU

ANIMALS

by

Alain Gree

illustrations by
Luis Camp

FRANKLIN WATTS

1 From larva to cockchafer

The female cockchafer lays its eggs in the soil. One month later each egg develops into a larva (like a fat white worm). After three years underground, the larva becomes a pupa, with a hard outer case. The next spring, the adult insect finally emerges.

2 From caterpillar to butterfly

The female butterfly lays its eggs on a leaf. A few weeks later, a small caterpillar (the larva) eats its way out of each egg shell. It eats the plant leaves almost non-stop until it is ready to pupate. The pupa hangs upside down from a plant until the adult butterfly appears.

3 From tadpole to frog

In the spring, the female frog lays its eggs (frogspawn) on a pond. After a while tiny tadpoles wriggle out of the jelly that surrounds the eggs. Over the next few months, as the tadpole gets bigger, four legs appear and its tail gets shorter. Bit by bit, the tadpole changes into a frog.

HOW DO
ANIMALS CHANGE?

A new-born puppy has two ears, four legs and a tail, just like a fully grown dog. As it grows older it gets bigger, but it keeps the same basic shape. Not all animals are born in the shape of a small adult. Many change their form completely as they develop: the caterpillar that turns into a butterfly, the tadpole that becomes a frog, and many more.

Nature is full of surprises. If you look carefully, you will be able to find some for yourselves, in the garden, in the countryside or beside a pond. It may be a tight bud that bursts into flower, or a nymph that splits open to free a dragonfly. There is always something to see, if you keep your eyes open!

HOW DO BEES MAKE HONEY?

Do you like toast and honey for tea? Bees make honey to feed their young larvae. By keeping bees in hives we can collect some of the honey.

Bees make honey from nectar, which is a sweet juice in the base of flowers. The insects fly from flower to flower and suck up the nectar through a long tube like a hollow tongue. They mix the nectar with juices from their mouth to make it into honey, which is then put into the little cells in the wax nest. The larvae eat some of it, and the rest is kept for the winter, when there are no flowers. It is the worker bees who make the honey, build the nest and look after the young – the larger queen bee lays the eggs, but leaves the rest of the work to the other bees in the colony.

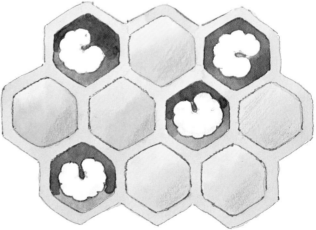

A bee's nest is made up of sheets of waxy cells, often called honeycombs. Both sides of the combs are covered with six-sided cells that fit neatly together. Some of the cells contain larvae, while others are full of honey.

7

THE FASTEST SPEED REACHED BY SOME ANIMALS

Snail
50 metres an hour

Tortoise
3 kilometres an hour

Octopus
6 kilometres an hour

Carp
12 kilometres an hour

Skylark
35 kilometres an hour

Rabbit
35 kilometres an hour

Crow
35 kilometres an hour

Elephant
40 kilometres an hour

Ostrich
50 kilometres an hour

Giraffe
55 kilometres an hour

Zebra
65 kilometres an hour

Coyote
65 kilometres an hour

Gazelle
80 kilometres an hour

Lion
85 kilometres an hour

Roe deer
95 kilometres an hour

Cheetah
100 kilometres an hour

WHICH ANIMALS ARE THE FASTEST?

Animals do not all move at the same speed. Some, like the boa constrictor, move as slowly as a tortoise. Others sometimes runs so fast that they could overtake a sports car. The biggest animals are not always the fastest: the hare can match the speed of a horse going at a gallop, and a dragonfly leaves the zebra way behind!

8

Crocodile
5 kilometres an hour

Pig
20 kilometres an hour

Sheep
25 kilometres an hour

Dog
30 kilometres an hour

Sea lion
0 kilometres an hour

Rhinoceros
45 kilometres an hour

Kangaroo
45 kilometres an hour

Whale
50 kilometres an hour

Horse
0 kilometres an hour

Hare
70 kilometres an hour

Stag
75 kilometres an hour

Dragonfly
80 kilometres an hour

350 kph in a dive

Peregrine falcon
0 kilometres an hour

Vulture
150 kilometres an hour

Eagle
160 kilometres an hour

Swift
170 kilometres an hour

How can you measure the speed of an animal? You measure the distance it covers in an hour. If it travels one kilometre, its speed is one kilometre an hour. If it travels 100 kilometres in the same time, its speed is 100 kilometres an hour. Find out your walking speed by walking for an hour and measuring the distance on a map.

The tallest animal
is the giraffe. It can be over six metres tall (about the same as a two-storey house).

The fastest dog
is the greyhound. It can run at up to 60 kilometres an hour.

The tallest bird
is the ostrich. Its head can reach up to 2.70 metres (as high as a single decker bus).

The heaviest animal
is the blue whale. It can be 33 metres long and weigh 180 tonnes (the weight of an airbus).

The fastest animal
is the peregrine falcon. In level flight it reaches 130 kilometres an hour, but it can dive at 350 kph (faster than a jet when it starts to land).

WHICH ANIMALS ARE CHAMPIONS?

Do you dream of one day being a champion, of beating a world record? Perhaps you would like to be the fastest runner, the best skier or the strongest swimmer. People hold all kinds of records, and so do animals. Some of them are quite amazing: the giraffe that can see over the tops of houses, for example, and the swan that flies at the same height as planes. Now find out about some other record holders in the world of animals...

The smallest bird
is the humming bird. I[t is?] six centimetres from b[eak] to tail and weighs le[ss] than two grammes ([the] same as an envelo[pe]).

The fastest bird
in level flight is the spine-tailed swift. It can fly at 170 kilometres an hour (the same as the top speed of some powerful cars).

The biggest dog
is the Saint Bernard. It can measure one metre tall at the shoulders and weigh 140 kilos (ten times the weight of the average dog).

The dog that jumps the highest
is the German shepherd dog. The record to beat: a wall 3.50 metres high (as high as a train).

The longest feathers
are found on the Japanese cockerel. The feathers can be more than 10 metres long (the same as a truck).

The highest-flying bird
is the swan. It flies in groups at up to 8,000 metres (airliners fly at the same altitude).

The oldest bird
is the cockatoo, which can live for up to 80 years (five times longer than most dogs).

The biggest fish
is the whale shark. It can be 18 metres long (the same as six windsurf boards), and weigh more than 40 tonnes (40 times heavier than a car).

11

Mayfly one day

Butterfly two months

Flea two months

Fly ten days

Cricket one year

Mouse five years

Hare eight years

Rabbit eight year

Nightingale 12 years

Cat 15 years

Sparrow 15 years

Frog 15 years

Bull 25 years

Horse 25 years

Eagle 30 years

Stork 35 years

Lion 50 years

Bear 50 years

Raven 50 years

Pike 70 years

HOW LONG DO THEY LIVE?

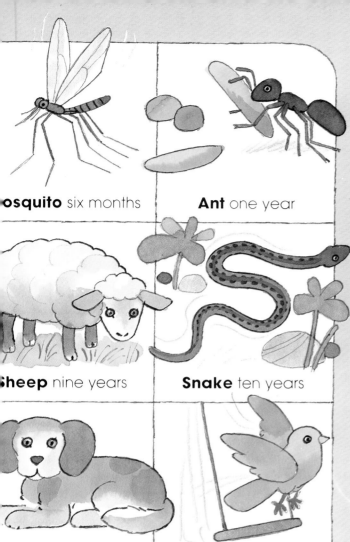

osquito six months

Ant one year

heep nine years

Snake ten years

Dog 15 years

Canary 17 years

Camel 40 years

Heron 50 years

ortoise 100 years

Parrot 70 years

Nature has more surprises in store! Did you know, for example, that a ten-year-old elephant is still quite young, whereas a butterfly is old after only two months? The wolf waits two years before it is adult, but a mosquito dies after only six months and the mayfly lives for just one day. You might like to guess how long the other animals on these pages can live for – cover up the answers with your hand while you think. Remember that these figures are a possible age for each animal. Many will die before they reach this age, while some may live for longer.

Elephants can live for 50 or 60 years

HOW DO BEAVERS BUILD?

This beaver family is hard at work building a new home in the middle of the river. First, the animals build a dam across the river, using mud and branches. Then they make their house, called a lodge, out of more branches, in the still water behind the dam. Beavers have very sharp front teeth for gnawing wood – they can cut down trees quite easily. They are good swimmers, too. They use their broad tail for steering. They swim into their lodge through underwater tunnels, where their nest is raised up above the water level.

air hole

branches

lodge

food

tunnel

Beavers first build an underwater platform out of mud and stones. Above that they make their lodge of branches, with an air hole in the top. Several tunnels lead into the lodge, which keeps them safe and warm in the middle of the river!

WHICH ANIMALS HIBERNATE?

Bears spend the winter in a cave or in the hollow trunk of a tree.

Marmots dig a burrow and sleep in family groups.

Dormice make a nest in which to sleep.

Hedgehogs roll up into a ball in a nest on the ground.

Lizards slide into a rocky crevice or under a tree root.

Carps bury themselves in mud.

Tortoises dig into soft earth and withdraw into their shell.

Snails find a hiding place and seal off the shell opening.

16

Frogs and **toads** settle down for the winter in some mud.

Grass snakes curl up in a pile of branches or under some logs.

Bees stay in their nests or hive all winter.

Crabs hide in muddy sand in a quiet spot by the sea.

Winter is a time of rest for many animals. Some even go into a kind of deep sleep in the autumn and do not wake up again until the spring. Animals that hibernate eat enough food in the summer to build up a store of body fat to last them through the long winter sleep.

Apart from bats, which spend the winter hanging upside down, most animals that hibernate sleep rolled up in a ball. They hide away somewhere warm and dark, perhaps in the ground, under a rock or in a pile of wood. Their body rests: the heart beats slower, their temperature drops and they hardly breathe. Little can disturb their sleep. Then, as the warm weather returns in spring, these animals come out of hibernation and become very active.

Some animals, like the squirrel, spend the winter in a half-sleep, waking up from time to time to nibble at food stored away the previous summer.

Pigeons carry messages to faraway places, and return home safely.

Guard dogs keep the burglars away.

Cows and goats provide milk, which can be made into delicious cheeses!

Sheep give us wool for knitting.

Sheepdogs look after flocks of sheep.

Hens lay eggs, which we can cook in so many ways.

Bees make honey, which tastes good at tea time!

Cats chase after mice in the attic or the cellar.

WHICH ANIMALS HELP US?

Animals have helped people for thousands of years. Dogs were the first animals to be used by man, for hunting in the Stone Age. Today, most dogs are kept as pets. Can you think of people who keep dogs as working animals? (You will find one answer on this page.)

Farm animals such as sheep and cows provide us with food, drink, and wool for clothes. Some animals pull carts or carry loads. But it is not only domesticated animals that help us. Wild animals, too, play an important part in our life. Which animals help you?

Guide dogs help blind people to find their way.

Horses carry people and pull carts and ploughs.

Silkworms spin a fine thread which can be used to make silk.

Toads help us by eating mosquitoes and other insects.

Hedgehogs help out in the garden by eating harmful creatures.

WHY DO WILD ANIMALS COME INTO TOWNS?

In recent years, certain wild animals have moved out of the countryside and into the town. You may not have seen them: they usually stay well hidden, in sewers, in sheds, on building sites, or at the bottom of the garden. Why have they left the woods and fields which are their proper home? For many, the place where people live is a place with plenty of food – even in winter! For others, the town provides an escape from their enemies or perhaps a good place to build a nest.

In sewers and cellars

The weasel comes out at night to hunt rats and mice.

The coypu, having escaped from fur farms, eats rubbish and root crops.

The brown rat, which can be brown or dark grey, often manages to avoid rat traps. It does a lot of damage by biting through telephone wires.

In parks and gardens

The hedgehog snuffles through the undergrowth at night in search of insects, slugs and snails.

Squirrels feed in and around trees.

The mole digs tunnels under the ground and pushes up piles of waste earth. Look out for molehills on lawns.

The badger hunts worms at night.

The bat feeds at night on flying insects.

The cricket and grasshopper can be heard 'singing' in the grass on summer days.

In buildings

The tawny owl may nest or roost in old buildings.

The redstart usually nests in a tree hole but in towns it will use a hole in a stone wall.

The swallow nests on a ledge or rafter in buildings.

Mice are common in buildings, where they steal food.

Scorpions are often found in hot countries. They hide in beds and under carpets.

In dustbins and on rubbish tips

The stone marten digs its den under garden sheds. It raids the dustbin and eats sparrows.

The fox usually hunts small animals, but in town eats all kinds of waste food.

Herring gulls often visit rubbish tips to scavenge for food scraps.

WHAT A MUDDLE!

Felix

Henry

George

Maxim

Alfred

The animals are busy collecting fruits for the winter. Look at the picture, then read the story. Can you find ten mistakes in the text?

Maxim is wearing a bowler hat, and a necklace round his neck. Henry is raking up strawberries with a red rake. George is pulling a cart full of pears. Alfred is carrying three blue pumpkins under his arms. As for Felix, he is happily picking chestnuts with his pickaxe.

Correct version: Maxim is wearing a cap (1), and a scarf (2) round his neck. Henry is raking up chestnuts (3) with a blue rake (4). George is pushing (5) a cart full of acorns (6). Alfred is carrying one (7) big orange (8) pumpkin on his head (9). As for Felix, he is happily picking chestnuts with his pitchfork (10).